W0115855

BIGHORN
SHEEP

Jack Ballard

FALCONGUIDES

GUILFORD, CONNECTICUT
HELENA, MONTANA

AN IMPRINT OF ROWMAN & LITTLEFIELD

An imprint of Rowman & Littlefield
Falcon, FalconGuides, and Outfit Your Mind are registered trademarks of Rowman & Littlefield.

Distributed by NATIONAL BOOK NETWORK

British Library Cataloguing-in-Publication Information is available on file.

Library of Congress Cataloging-in-Publication Data is available on file.

ISBN 978-0-7627-8491-2 (paperback)

♾™ The paper used in this publication meets the minimum requirements of American National Standard for Information Sciences—Permanence of Paper for Printed Library Materials, ANSI/NISO Z39.48-1992.

This book is dedicated to my son, Micah, our many shared outdoor adventures, and a bighorn ram.

Contents

Contents

Chapter 6: Bighorn Sheep and Other Animals

Chapter 7: Bighorn Sheep and Humans

Acknowledgments

Several wildlife professionals have expanded my understanding of bighorn sheep and provided valuable information for this book and my other writings on bighorns. They are: Dr. Bob Garrott, Professor of Ecology at Montana State University; Shawn Stewart, Wildlife Biologist with the Montana Department of Fish, Wildlife & Parks; Doug McWhirter, Wildlife Biologist with the Wyoming Game & Fish Department; and Hank Edwards, Wildlife Disease Specialist with the Wyoming Game & Fish Department. I am especially grateful to Melanie Woolever, National Bighorn Sheep Program Leader, of the United States Forest Service for reviewing and making helpful suggestions on the manuscript.

Swarovski Optics has generously supplied superb binoculars to support my field observations of wildlife. Thank you!

Introduction

On a November elk hunt several decades ago, my older brother and I found ourselves sliding downward from an exceedingly high ridge on the flank of the Madison Range in Montana. Cresting a bulge on the vertiginous slope, the sight of three animals in a tiny, open basin found us scrambling for our binoculars. My initial impression of the animals assumed a small herd of mule deer, but even before I peered through my binoculars, I knew what they were. Three lordly bighorn rams lounged in the snow, the brown coats on their muscular bodies appearing thick and sleek under the midday sun. Their horns were much lighter, massive, and arcing from their heads like fence posts bent into a circle. The rams failed to detect our approach from above, allowing us to sneak within a distance of perhaps half a city block from the nearest sheep.

For some time we watched them in silence. I can still recall their white nose patches and the pale fur on their rumps, the grinding of their molars as they chewed their cud, and the dark, cloven hooves at the end of their outstretched front legs. Beyond the rams the landscape peeled away in an emerald mosaic of timber and an endless chain of barren mountain peaks melding into an ageless blue sky. The wildness of the space and the strength of life that seemed to radiate from the lounging bighorns will remain with me until erased by death or dementia.

Despite their apparent virility, bighorns are fragile creatures. They snort at -30°F temperatures, yet have less resistance to certain respiratory diseases than a newborn human. Perhaps more than any other species of hoofed mammal in North America, they need the care of thoughtful people to survive. After reading this book, I hope you'll be amply motivated to do your part.

CHAPTER 1 Names and Faces

Names and Visual Description

Bighorn sheep are creatures of the mountains and may also inhabit rough, badland regions of the plains. Their overall appearance is brown, varying from hues of rich chocolate to reddish or golden brown, depending on the region the animal inhabits and the time of year. Bighorns have stout, blocky bodies. Their tails are brown and stubby, and are only easily observed by the unaided eye from the rear at close range. The rump of the bighorn looks large, partly due to its highly developed muscles but also enhanced by its distinct coloration. In contrast to the brown body of the sheep, the rump appears cream-colored or pure white. Bighorns also have a pale patch of fur on the end of their nose, and varying levels of lighter fur on the inside of their legs and belly.

Although "sheep" in the truest sense of the word (bighorns can actually mate with domestic sheep in controlled conditions), observers expecting the long, woolly coat of the domestic sheep on a bighorn are mistaken. The bighorn's fur is sleek and much shorter than that of a domestic sheep. In late winter their coats may fade considerably. Their fur becomes patchy when shedding in the spring and early summer, but for most of the year, their haircoat looks sleek and well-groomed.

Both female and male bighorn sheep have horns. The horns of a mature male dwarf those of a female. The horns grow from the top of the head and curl out and backward. Exceptionally large males may have horns that spiral into a full circle when viewed from the side.

American Indians inhabiting what is now the western portion of the United States utilized bighorn sheep for food and other purposes. Various tribes had different names for the sheep. The Blackfeet of northwestern Montana referred to the bighorn as "big head." The Mandans of the Dakotas called the animal "big horn," while the Crees of western Canada referred to the species as

Bighorn sheep are named for the massive, spiraling horns found on males of the species.

"ugly reindeer." Early European trappers and explorers sometimes adopted the names of the native peoples for bighorn sheep, but naturalists were often confused about the specific identity of the animal.

Such was the case with members of the Lewis and Clark expedition. The captains were aware of the presence of bighorns before they encountered or killed one, based on verbal accounts from other explorers and a spoon Clark observed in a village of Teton Sioux fashioned from the horn of a bighorn sheep. On May 25, 1805, Clark killed a female bighorn in the bluffs along the Missouri River in eastern Montana. The captain described the animal as "a female ibex or big horn animal," reflecting some of the confusion that surrounded the species in his day. Some American naturalists believed bighorns were a type of ibex, goatlike creatures that are native to central Europe, Asia, and northern Africa. Others believed them to be a strain of argali, wild sheep indigenous to eastern Asia. The confusion in the minds of Lewis and Clark is evident on their maps. In eastern Montana they named two separate watercourses "Argalia Creek" and "Ibex Creek" in the region where they first encountered bighorn sheep.

On Clark's eastward (return) journey down the Yellowstone River, he encountered a major tributary known by the Crow Indians as the "Bighorn River," the name he adopted on his map which persists today. After decades of confusion in the nineteenth century regarding the river's namesake animal, biologists successfully differentiated bighorn sheep from the argali and ibex of yonder continents and agreed upon the name "bighorn sheep," which the animals carry today. The scientific name for bighorn sheep is *Ovis canadensis*.

Related Species in North America

Bighorn sheep share summer and winter range with several other species of hoofed mammals, including elk, mule deer, and mountain goats. They may also be occasionally found in the proximity of moose and whitetail deer. Bighorns are kin to the "thin-horned" sheep of North America, the Dall's and Stone's sheep of northwestern Canada and Alaska.

Stone's and Dall's sheep are very close relatives to bighorn sheep—so close, in fact, that they have been successfully crossbred in captivity. However, the ranges of these northern-dwelling sheep and bighorns do not overlap, although both species exist in the mountains of British Columbia, Canada. In contrast to

Bighorn sheep are close relatives of Dall's and Stone's sheep that live in more northern habitats than bighorns. SHUTTERSTOCK

bighorns, Dall's sheep are completely white. Stone's sheep, technically a subspecies of Dall's sheep that inhabit the southern portion of its range, are found most abundantly in northern British Columbia. Compared to bighorns their coloration is more grayish than brown. While some Stone's sheep have a dark, solid charcoal appearance, most have a more mottled gray-brown coat. The horns of Dall's and Stone's sheep are somewhat thinner than those found on bighorn sheep, and tend to flare farther from the head as well.

In portions of their range in the western United States, bighorn sheep are found in proximity to mountain goats. Early European hunters and naturalists sometimes confused the identities of mountain goats and bighorns if they hadn't encountered both species. Once both animals had been viewed, they quickly realized they were seeing two different creatures.

The overall creamy-white appearance of the mountain goat contrasts sharply with the brown body of the bighorn sheep. Mountain goats sometimes exhibit a dirty coat of dingy gray, but are still lighter than bighorns. The fur of a mountain goat is longer than that of a bighorn sheep, especially in the cold months of the year when adorned in their winter coat. In comparison to the sleek coat of a bighorn, mountain goats appear shaggy. Like sheep, both male and female mountain goats have horns. However, their horns are colored and shaped differently than those on a bighorn. The smooth horns of a mountain goat are black, with bases that sometimes appear as gray when soiled. Their horns sweep up and back from the top of the head, ending in sharp, daggerlike points. In contrast, the horns of bighorn sheep are tan or auburn in color, slightly rough in appearance, and not nearly as pointed as those on a mountain goat.

Bighorn sheep also share habitat with several members of the deer family in some locations. Compared to moose or elk, bighorns are much smaller. Moose are darker in color and have much longer legs than a bighorn. Elk are also taller and heavier than bighorns, and their coats generally appear lighter and more reddish or golden brown than a bighorn. The neck of an elk is much longer. Female elk have neither horns nor antlers; male elk have antlers that are bony protrusions from the head, unlike the curling horns of a bighorn.

From a distance, mule deer may be the animal most likely confused for a bighorn sheep. They are roughly similar in size. Like bighorns, mule deer exhibit a light rump patch, and in the summer a mule deer's coat may be light brown or reddish in appearance. However, several details easily distinguish these species. First, a mule deer has a leaner, athletic look and longer neck than a bighorn. The name "mule deer" hearkens to their oversize ears that are much larger than those of a bighorn. Like elk, mule deer either have antlers if they are male, or lack horns or antlers if female.

Subspecies of Bighorn Sheep

Animals that inhabit range that is isolated from other populations of the same species often develop physical and/or behavioral characteristics that are different from other members of their own kind. For example, southern populations of many species are smaller than those in the north. Their coloration may differ as well. Regional variations within a species have led biologists to identify these different groups as subspecies.

In the twentieth century many naturalists were nearly subspecies crazy, sometimes identifying a dozen or more subspecies of a single North American mammal. Currently most biologists are much more conservative in their delineation of these distinct population groups. In most cases the number of subspecies for large mammal species on the continent has been whittled from many to a few. Such is the case with bighorn sheep. At various periods in history, as many as seven subspecies of bighorn sheep have been identified in North America.

Today most biologists recognize two or three subspecies of bighorns, while some might argue there is but a single species with no subspecies at all. Subspecies designations are sometimes muddled when biological and management classifications differ. Such is the case with bighorn sheep in the United States.

Desert bighorn sheep, like this ram in Utah's Zion National Park, are a subspecies especially adapted to living in arid environments. They are slightly smaller than Rocky Mountain bighorns. SHUTTERSTOCK

The two subspecies most commonly identified with bighorn sheep are the Rocky Mountain bighorn sheep (*Ovis canadensis canadensis*) and the desert bighorn sheep (*Ovis canadensis nelsoni*). The Rocky Mountain subspecies ranges across portions of western Canada and the western United States as far south as New Mexico. Desert bighorns are found in the southwestern United States. Occupied states include Utah, Nevada, Arizona, New Mexico, western Texas, and southern California, with a growing population also found in southwestern Colorado.

Distinguishing between Rocky Mountain and desert bighorns based on appearance alone is a difficult (some would argue impossible) task. In general, desert bighorns are thought to be smaller and exhibit a lighter coloration than their Rocky Mountain counterparts. Some believe the horns on female desert bighorns are longer than those on the Rocky Mountain subspecies. The horns of rams on the southern subspecies may be longer but less massive than those found on northern animals.

In some biological circles a third subspecies of bighorn sheep is theorized, the California bighorn sheep (*Ovis canadensis california*). This subspecies is identified as those sheep historically occupying range west of the Rocky Mountains, including the Sierra Nevada of California and the Cascade Range in Oregon, Washington, and British Columbia. California bighorn males are thought to have smaller skulls and smaller, more widely flaring horns than Rocky Mountain bighorns. Whether these characteristics and geographical separation from most Rocky Mountain bighorn populations warrant subspecies classification remains a matter of debate among biologists.

When management and conservation enter the picture, the subspecies designations for bighorn sheep become even more muddled. The United States Fish & Wildlife Service (USFWS) has designated two population segments of bighorn sheep occurring in California with special status. The first is the population of desert bighorn sheep occupying the Peninsular Ranges in southern California from the San Jacinto Mountains south to the United States–Mexico border, and Baja California, Mexico. These are called Penisular bighorn sheep by the USFWS and are technically known as a Distinct Population Segment (DPS), not a separate subspecies. Under the provisions of the Endangered Species Act (ESA), geographically isolated populations of a species can be given status as an endangered species. Such is the case with the Peninsular bighorn sheep that were declared an endangered species via their status as a DPS in 1998.

The bighorn sheep subspecies discussion becomes even more convoluted in relation to the Sierra Nevada bighorn sheep (*Ovis canadensis sierrae*), a subspecies designated by the USFWS in 2008. In 2000 bighorn sheep in California's Sierra Nevada were granted endangered species protection by the USFWS after their population crashed to a low of around 125 animals. At this time the bighorns of the Sierra Nevada were considered representatives of the California bighorn sheep subspecies as described above. Utilizing research indicating that the bighorns found in the Sierra are more closely aligned genetically with animals of the southwestern deserts than the northern mountains, but genetically different in some ways from both, the USFWS officially concluded these animals were a separate subspecies and named them Sierra Nevada bighorn sheep. However, a change in subspecies designation by a federal agency does not automatically make its decision accepted science, and not all biologists specializing in the natural history of North American wild sheep would agree with the position of the USFWS.

To conclude the subspecies discussion, it is interesting to note that some biologists would prefer to regard all bighorn sheep as members of a single species, no subspecies included. These scientists point out that historically interchanges between all populations now regarded as subspecies occurred on the edges of their range. They might further argue that even the most expert observer would be hard-pressed to identify individual animals as belonging to a particular subspecies in the absence of its known geographical range. Neither size nor horn shape, two physical characteristics often related to subspecies distinctions in bighorn males, is consistent. Small mature males from the Rocky Mountain subspecies on poor range may be similar in size to large desert males. The flaring horns offered as a physical characteristic of the California bighorn sheep subspecies are sometimes observed on Rocky Mountain animals. I have personally observed bighorn males in Montana with flaring horns that could easily be taken for the California subspecies.

If one wishes to push the issue even further, some biologists admit that all wild sheep of North America, both the bighorn and thin-horned varieties, might legitimately be classified as a single species, since they can interbreed and produce fertile, functional offspring.

Physical Characteristics

Bighorn sheep are not particularly tall or heavy animals. They are considered medium-size ungulates in comparison to others in

Identifying subspecies of bighorn sheep based on physical characteristics is nearly impossible. These Rocky Mountain rams are of similar age but show different coat colors and horn shapes.

North America. Average weights for bighorn males and females are comparable to those of the whitetail or mule deer. The overall dimensions of bighorns (height at the shoulder, overall length) are also similar between bighorns and deer.

Adult bighorn males normally stand from 2.5 to 3.5 feet at the shoulder, with a head-to-tail body length ranging from 5.2 to 6.1 feet. Males commonly weigh from 130 to 275 pounds. Females are substantially smaller, with normal weights varying from 80 to 150 pounds. Adult mass among bighorns is usually determined by habitat quality. Sheep with access to increased amounts of nutritious forage maximize body weight, while those in marginal

habitats obtain smaller sizes as adults. An exceptionally large male weighing 301 pounds was once surveyed by biologists in Jasper National Park in Alberta, Canada.

Nomenclature for gender in bighorn sheep follows that of domestic sheep. Adult males are called "rams"; females are referred to as "ewes." Newborns or young of the year are known as "lambs."

Horns and Horn Development

Perhaps the most remarkable and distinguishing feature of the bighorn sheep is the massive, curling horns carried by an adult ram. The horns may weigh up to 30 pounds or slightly more, sometimes exceeding 10 percent of the animal's total weight. On the average, bighorn sheep horns increase in mass as one travels from south to north within their range. In the 1990s a number of rams were harvested by hunters in western Montana with horns measuring over 17 inches in circumference at the base of the horn near the skull. Measured from the base of the horn where it touches the skull around the outside curl, bighorn rams have been recorded with horns measuring over 49 inches in length.

The horns of bighorns are actually composed of keratin fibers, similar to the horns adorning other animals such as mountain goats, impala, bison, ibex, and some strains of domestic cattle. Keratin is the material also found in hair, hooves, and human fingernails. The horns of bighorn sheep form around bony projections on the top of a ram's skull known as "horn cores." Horns on bighorn sheep begin growing shortly after birth, and by its first birthday a bighorn ram may have horns that are 5 to 8 inches in length.

Each year another horn sheath grows from the horn core. The new sheath develops inside the previous horn sheath, expanding it and forcing it farther away from the horn core, which increases both the length and the circumference of the horn. A ram's horn is thus a succession of horn sheaths stacked one inside of the next, similar to a bunch of empty ice-cream cones or paper cups placed

Horns on bighorn sheep grow from the time the animal is born. Within a few months the horns on this lamb photographed in Badlands National Park, South Dakota, will be visible.
SHUTTERSTOCK

one inside another. What is viewed on the outside of the horn is only the exposed portion of each horn sheath.

The annual development of a ram's horns creates a dark indentation where each new horn sheath begins to develop. These indentations create discernible growth rings, or annuli, that can be used to estimate a ram's age. Problems arise in this aging method for several reasons. First, rams may break off the entire sheath grown in the first year of life (sometimes known as "lamb tips") when fighting or rubbing their horns against trees. In extreme cases rams may lose up to three years of horn growth when the ends of the horns splinter in battle. Horns damaged in such a way are said to be "broomed." In such cases the total of the annuli is less than the ram's actual age.

Another aging problem arises in relation to the annuli found between the ram's first and second year. On many sheep this growth ring is less distinct than those found between successive horn sheaths. Additionally, some animals develop false growth rings. The horns of all bighorn sheep are rippled and indented in appearance. Extreme indentations are sometimes very difficult to distinguish from true annuli.

The length of a bighorn ram's horn increases most rapidly in the first years of life. Horns may lengthen at a rate of 6 inches per year for the first four years of life. Once a ram reaches nine years of age, its horns seldom add more than 2 inches of length from the base per year.

Development of the smaller horns found on ewes follows the same biological pattern as the massive horns carried by rams. Annuli on ewe horns are harder to distinguish due to their smaller size. Unlike the horns of rams that may be broomed fighting, the horns of ewes generally remain intact.

The horns of bighorn sheep develop dark lines know as annuli. Each line represents one year of growth. SHUTTERSTOCK

CHAPTER 2 Range and Habitat

North American Range—Historic

The occupied range of bighorn sheep has contracted dramatically since European settlers arrived in North America. Bighorn sheep, like elk, are now most strongly associated with the Rocky Mountains. However, unlike elk that once roamed over much of what is now the contiguous United States, the historic range of bighorn sheep was always confined to the western half of the continent. The reason for this is quite simple: Bighorns are animals of the open country. They do not live in dense forests. The eastern woodlands of the continent have thus never been home to bighorns.

Historically bighorn sheep occupied suitable habit as far south as the southern reaches of Baja California and northwestern

Bighorn sheep were historically found in some habitats on the plains. This ram was photographed in the breaks along the Missouri River in eastern Montana.

Mexico. In the United States, a line drawn from the "Big Bend" of the Rio Grande in Texas northward to the intersection of the eastern border of Saskatchewan and North Dakota roughly approximates the eastern edge of the bighorn's historic range. They occupied mountainous areas jutting northward into Canada along the Rocky Mountains, primarily in southwestern Alberta and southeastern British Columbia. On the western side, the original range of bighorn sheep did not extend into the dense coastal forests of Washington, Oregon, and California. Bighorns ranged in drier, more open habitats in the interior mountains of these states.

Although bighorn sheep are sometimes called "mountain monarchs," such a nickname tends to overlook the fact that historically the animals were creatures of the prairies as well as the mountains. Bighorn sheep were found in plains habitats in areas where steep slopes or cliffs gave them escape cover from predators. These places were often found along eroded river corridors, such as the breaks along the Missouri River, where Lewis and Clark first encountered bighorn sheep on their westward trek to the Pacific Ocean. Indigenous bands of bighorns tracked the soils of western North and South Dakota and western Nebraska, although most contemporary Americans do not conceive of them in such habitats.

Bighorn sheep faced the same perils from European homesteaders as other large ungulates and predators. They were killed for meat and for sport, the large, impressive horns of the rams considered a desirable trophy by hunters, including the great conservationist and president, Theodore Roosevelt. The meat of bighorn sheep has a delicate flavor, motivating early hunters to target them for their taste.

Hunting took a dramatic toll on bighorn sheep numbers in the later decades of the nineteenth century and early twentieth century, but other factors whittled their numbers as well. Domestic cattle and other livestock grazed on pastures in the foothills of the Rocky Mountains, leaving little for the mouths of bighorn sheep during the winter, sheep that often migrated to the mountaintops during the summer but passed the winter in the lowlands.

Competition for forage wasn't the greatest threat facing bighorn sheep from the newly arrived livestock of homesteaders. Diseases and parasites carried by domestic sheep are easily transmitted to bighorns. Lacking the immunity domestic sheep had developed during their centuries of domestication, bighorn populations in many areas were decimated by diseases from domestic livestock. To this day, disease transmission from domestic to wild sheep is one of the greatest perils to bighorn populations, and on numerous bighorn ranges wildlife managers have worked diligently to keep wild sheep separated from their domestic kin.

How many bighorn sheep inhabited North America before the historic collapse in their population? No one knows for sure. In 1929, in his book titled *Lives of Game Animals*, Ernest Thompson Seton estimated there were 4 million bighorn sheep in North America prior to their decimation, 2 million in the contiguous United States and another 2 million in Canada. Seton's estimate has been widely accepted, although other biologists argue

Fur trappers and explorers hunted bighorn sheep, finding the greatest success when targeting sheep on winter range. LISA BALLARD

that the bighorn sheep population in North America has never climbed beyond 500,000 animals. However, eyewitness accounts from early explorers with a reputation for competence and accuracy point to abundance in many habitats.

Osborne Russell, a fur trapper, kept a journal while rambling through the Rocky Mountains from 1834 to 1843. He frequently notes that he and his companions, or the American Indians that they encountered, hunted bighorn sheep. He describes bighorns in terms of abundance in numerous places in his journals, and while in the mountains of northwestern Wyoming wrote that "thousands of mountain sheep were scattered up and down feeding on the short grass which grew among the cliffs and crevices."

Bighorns were the meal of choice for many early hunters, and the scant historical records of their presence in the nineteenth century indicate there were plenty to be found. For example, bighorns were abundant enough in the Southwest that sheep meat was available in markets in Tucson, Arizona, in the early decades of the twentieth century. An annual report from Yellowstone National Park in 1877 indicates nearly 2,000 sheep were killed in the region by hunters who pursued animals for their hides. Many biologists believe that bighorn sheep were the most abundant animal in the mountains of Idaho in the early 1800s.

However, despite their apparent abundance in places, unregulated hunting, habitat loss, parasites, and diseases were driving bighorn sheep to extinction over vast segments of their historic range. Their presence on the western prairies of North and South Dakota ended by 1905. They disappeared from California's Yosemite National Park around 1914. In eastern Montana, where Lewis and Clark first encountered them, a ram killed in 1916 is thought to be the last confirmed sighting of a bighorn sheep in the state's prairie habitat. Ernest Thompson Seton wrote in 1929 that bighorns were extirpated from the Black Hills of South Dakota in 1899. E. R. Hall, a naturalist who documented the mammals of Nevada in a book published in 1946, declared that bighorns were extinct in the state. In 1906 the State Game Warden of Idaho reported that a mere 300 to 400 bighorns were estimated to occupy the entire state.

North American Range—Current

Relegated to remnants of their historic range, most states where bighorns continued to exist banned their hunting around the turn of the twentieth century. However, disease and habitat loss continued to plague sheep herds even in the absence of hunting.

After World War II a number of states began transplanting bighorns from healthy herds into previously occupied habitats from which they had been eliminated. Sheep returned to several states where indigenous bands had been completely wiped out. Numerous transplants were successful, resulting in the establishment of bighorns over increasingly broad portions of their native range. However, some transplanted animals failed to thrive in their new environments, and the introduced bighorns eventually died out. As of 1990 researchers had documented over 200 bighorn sheep transplants to their native range undertaken by fourteen different state wildlife agencies.

Bighorns, including this young ram in Joshua Tree National Park, California, range over tens of thousands of acres of desert habitat in the southwestern United States. SHUTTERSTOCK

At the present time, bighorn sheep occupy fifteen states and two Canadian provinces, Alberta and British Columbia. Desert bighorns also roam across parts of Mexico, including limited areas in the extreme northwestern portion of the mainland, and on the Baja Peninsula.

In the United States, bighorn sheep are found in the following states, with some states inhabited by members of one or more recognized subspecies: Arizona, California, Colorado, Idaho, Montana, Nebraska, Nevada, New Mexico, North Dakota, Oregon, South Dakota, Texas, Utah, Washington, and Wyoming.

Cataloging the exact regional locations of bighorn sheep herds in each state is beyond the scope of this book. Suffice it to say that depending on the state, sheep have remained in, or returned to, varying percentages of their original habitat. In most states, wildlife managers have identified specific populations units, or herds, of bighorns that are separated from other

Bighorn sheep were never eliminated from the mountains of northwestern Wyoming, including the Wind River Range, home of this ewe and lamb. SHUTTERSTOCK

members of their kind, most often by natural geographic or man-made barriers. Man-made barriers include fenced highways that sheep are unable to cross or habitat corridors now occupied by domestic livestock, croplands, or human inhabitation. These human-induced obstacles often impede genetic interchange between herds and prohibit sheep from expanding their range into unoccupied areas. Arizona, for example, has over thirty distinct herds or population units of desert bighorns, and a single herd of Rocky Mountain bighorns located in the east-central portion of the state. Where disease might be transmitted from one herd to another, wildlife managers sometimes deliberately attempt to limit interchange between bighorn sheep herds.

Some states have but a few population units of bighorns. Texas has around a half-dozen herds of desert bighorns. South Dakota's sheep are found in just four major herds, totaling around 300 animals in 2013. To the north, North Dakota's sheep also numbered around 300 animals in the same time period, bighorns also confined to just a few population units. Nebraska's bighorns number around 340 animals in five herds.

Other states have relatively high numbers of bighorn sheep, creatures that occupy significant portions of their native range. Bighorns were never extirpated from Colorado. Intact herds and an aggressive transplanting program conducted since 1945 have increased the number of population units of Rocky Mountain bighorns to around eighty, with a handful of desert bighorn herds located in the west-central part of the state. Some 500 desert bighorns track Colorado; Rocky Mountain bighorns number nearly 7,000.

Northwestern Wyoming holds some of the most impressive herds of bighorns. Bighorn sheep were never extirpated from the Gros Ventre, Wind River, and Absaroka mountain ranges. The herds now inhabiting these areas have never been supplemented with sheep from other locations, making them true native survivors in the high country. In the sprawling Absaroka Range, over 4,000 bighorn sheep exist in one extended, connected population, many in bands that number just a few dozen animals.

No matter where they're found, bighorn sheep populations in the contiguous United States are fraught with frailty. Tough animals capable of withstanding bitter cold and extreme drought, catastrophic disease events frequently decimate entire herds, leading to what biologists call "all-age die-offs." An acute disease outbreak may take 80 percent or more of the sheep from a population unit. In some cases the remainder are so compromised that they fail to reproduce and eventually fade from existence. Understanding and managing disease among bighorns is perhaps the most critical factor in determining what their range will be in the future.

Bighorn Sheep Habitat

Bighorn sheep may be found in the mountains, the plains, or the desert. But within these vastly different ecosystems, several commonalities determine suitable sheep habitat. First, bighorns prefer open areas. Visual detection of predators and the ability to flee

Open, rocky environments, like those found in Zion National Park, Utah, give bighorns the ability to see and flee effectively from predators. SHUTTERSTOCK

are critical to survival. Thus, bighorns range in areas where vegetation is neither too tall nor too thick to see clearly at a distance. Research indicates sheep are seldom found on gentle or moderate slopes where trees and shrubs cover more than 25 percent of the area. They also avoid brushy places where shrubs are more than 2 feet tall. On steep slopes they may venture into locations with somewhat heavier cover, but favor sparse vegetation at or above their line of sight in all environments.

Bighorns sometimes move through timbered areas on migrations or at other times, but do so with an apparent sense of danger. They tend to move quickly when traveling through forested habitats. Research on wild sheep has shown that their heart rate increases substantially when they enter forested habitats, attesting to the discomfort they experience in confined environments limiting their sight. Open timber is sometimes used by bighorns, but they are extremely reluctant to enter dense cover.

Another characteristic of bighorn sheep habitat consistent from alpine to arid ecosystems involves escape terrain. Bighorns are remarkably adept at traversing steep slopes and cliff faces. When danger threatens, sheep dash to the security of terrain where predators follow them with great difficulty or abandon the chase. Prairie badlands, canted mountain slopes, bluffs, rimrocks, and cliffs offer security to bighorns. Research indicates Rocky Mountain bighorn sheep are seldom found more than 0.5 mile from such escape terrain. Some research has shown that Rocky Mountain bighorns on winter range spend over 80 percent of their time within 110 yards of rocky terrain in which they can elude predators. Biologists have concluded that suitable escape terrain is a critical habitat component for bighorn sheep, something without which they cannot survive.

Water is another important component of bighorn sheep habitat, especially in desert environments. Bighorns obtain water from plant matter and dew, but may also eat snow. They are typically found within 1 mile of some type of surface water, be it a stream, pond, or spring. Sheep sometimes occupy habitat as far as 2 miles from a water source. Desert bighorns have an astonishing capacity

PARKS, WILDERNESS, AND THE CONTINUATION OF THE SPECIES

Were it not for remote, inhospitable areas where they found refuge from human hunters and a buffer from the diseases carried by domestic sheep, bighorns may have been driven to extinction. National parks, where they received protection from hunting and existed away from domestic animals, were important reserves for bighorns in earlier times. Some prime examples of national parks important to the historical survival of bighorns include Yellowstone National Park in northwestern Wyoming, Rocky Mountain National Park in central Colorado, and Glacier National Park in northwestern Montana.

The passage of the Wilderness Act of 1964 created vast tracts of pristine habitat off-limits to vehicles, timber harvest, and other activities that disrupt and displace bighorn sheep. Domestic sheep grazed many wilderness areas in the past as one of these areas' legal uses, but the grazing allotments in some have been retired, giving bighorns a buffer from disease. However, a high percentage of bighorns are found on national forest and Bureau of Land Management (BLM) lands lacking wilderness protections. A variety of land-use practices on these public lands (grazing by domestic livestock, motorized recreation, and energy development) are

to exist for extended periods without drinking. In extreme cases they may go up to fourteen days without water in dry seasons. However, some source of water is essential to their survival. Restoration efforts of desert bighorn sheep in many places have focused upon the construction of cisterns to catch rainwater or the development of seeps and springs to provide more water. When

direct threats to the continuation of the species in the contiguous United States. Wilderness areas and national parks continue to be very important refuges for bighorn sheep, although they nurture but a small percentage of the bighorns roaming public lands in the Lower 48.

The following national parks hold bighorn sheep. Some populations noted are transient and may spend significant amounts of time outside of park boundaries.

PARK	STATE
Grand Canyon National Park	Arizona
Death Valley National Park	California
Joshua Tree National Park	California
Sequoia–Kings Canyon National Park	California
Yosemite National Park	California
Rocky Mountain National Park	Colorado
Glacier National Park	Montana
Theodore Roosevelt National Park	North Dakota
Badlands National Park	South Dakota
Arches National Park	Utah
Canyonlands National Park	Utah
Capitol Reef National Park	Utah
Zion National Park	Utah
North Cascades National Park	Washington
Grand Teton National Park	Wyoming
Yellowstone National Park	Wyoming

watering, bighorns show the same need for unimpeded vision and proximity to escape cover as at other times. Water sources surrounded by high vegetation or much farther than 0.25 mile from escape cover are seldom used by bighorns.

In mountainous areas many bands of bighorn sheep often occupy different habitat during the summer and winter. Summer

National parks are important refuges for bighorn sheep. This magnificent ram finds excellent habitat in Glacier National Park, Montana. SHUTTERSTOCK

finds them high in the mountains, grazing on alpine ridgetops where the elevation often exceeds 10,000 feet above sea level. During the winter these sheep descend to the foothills where snow cover is shallower and cured grasses from the previous summer provide forage. Some hearty bighorns in the Rocky Mountains spend their entire life in the alpine zone. These animals winter on very high ridges where the piercing winter winds clear the vegetation of snow. The winter range of these animals typically occurs on south-facing slopes where sun exposure warms their bodies and hastens snowmelt. All bighorns are remarkable animals, but many naturalists believe those sheep that winter on 10,000-foot ridgetops are the most extraordinary of all.

CHAPTER 3 Nutritional Requirements and Forage

Nutritional Requirements

Much less is known about the specific nutritional requirements of bighorn sheep in comparison to more intensively studied ungulates such as elk and whitetail deer. Captive bighorns have been recorded eating an average of 3 pounds of plant material per day, but the extent to which this intake approximates the rate of wild sheep isn't clearly understood.

Like other hoofed mammals wintering in cold climates, bighorn sheep lower their nutritional intake during the winter. While it seems the animals would graze or browse more during the

When forage quality is low during the winter, bighorns save energy by resting more and feeding less. LISA BALLARD

winter because it takes more energy to stay warm in the cold, a different survival strategy is at work. Eating is an activity that burns energy in excess of what an animal requires in a resting state. One study found that bighorn sheep burned slightly over 30 percent more energy feeding than they did resting. Winter forage is typically of much lower quality than food items found on summer range. Burning substantial amounts of energy to ingest low-quality forage is a poor survival strategy. Thus, bighorns tend to rest more and get by on less feed in the winter than the summer.

The nutritional value of forage on a bighorn sheep's range is believed to influence a number of health-related factors in sheep herds. Ewes on range that provides poor nutrition do not have as high reproductive rates as those finding abundant, high-quality forage. Nutritional stress is also thought to be a potential influence in susceptibility to disease. Sheep unable to find enough

Access to reliable water sources is an important feature in bighorn sheep habitat. Bighorns will rarely be found more than a mile from some type of surface water. SHUTTERSTOCK

suitable forage to meet their nutritional demands may succumb to diseases unable to overpower well-fed bighorns.

In addition to the forage required for energy and bodily maintenance, bighorn sheep, like other living creatures, need water to survive. Lakes, streams, springs, and other sources of surface water provide sheep most of their water demands in the majority of their habitats. However, bighorns may also obtain water from moisture contained in plants, snow, and ice. The ability of desert bighorn sheep to endure extended periods without water rivals that of most animals humans associate with existence in arid environments, such as the camel. Researchers have found that desert bighorns may not drink for periods up to two weeks long, sometimes losing 20 percent of their normal body weight due to dehydration.

Like camels, desert bighorns can restore water in the body in a single stint of consumption. A researcher measuring water consumption of desert bighorns in California documented a ram consuming 4.94 gallons of water in a single drinking episode, approximately 23 percent of his body weight. Other bighorns were recorded consuming up to 20 percent of their body weight in water after extended bouts of dehydration. Some biologists believe bighorns can exist for extended periods of time without any access to surface water at all, deriving enough moisture from plant matter to survive. If this is the case, it most likely applies to very few locations containing small herds of sheep.

Digestion

The digestive process begins with food intake. Bighorn sheep have developed the ability to ingest comparatively large amounts of forage in a hurry. This adaptation decreases the time they need to spend feeding. Feeding activity requires them to be less alert and may lead them away from rocky escape cover, two factors that increase their vulnerability to predators.

Bighorns frequently feed upon coarse, woody plants and tough, dry grass. A bighorn's front teeth are quite sharp, their rear teeth large and strong. A sheep's teeth grow throughout its entire life to counteract the wear involved in eating. Like other ruminants, bighorn sheep have a long, complex digestive system with a stomach composed of four chambers. Bighorns don't chew their forage while eating. Rather, it's bitten off and swallowed rapidly. After feeding, sheep retreat to secure areas where they lay down, or "bed," during the day. At this time they regurgitate food that has entered the first chamber of their stomach. It is then chewed thoroughly, re-swallowed, and passes through the remainder of the digestive tract. The digestive system of bighorn sheep is particularly efficient in digesting dry plant matter.

Food Sources

Ungulate species fall on a continuum between browsers and grazers. Browsers, like moose, generally specialize in the consumption of plant matter found on trees and shrubs. Leaves, twigs, buds, and evergreen needles compose a very high percentage of a browser's annual diet. Grazers, on the other hand, eat mostly grass. Animals like bison specialize in the consumption of grasses and other leafy plants known as forbs. They seldom feed on shrubs or trees. Some species, like elk, are generalist feeders that are happy to browse or graze, depending on the food sources available on their range. This explains why elk can be found in such diverse areas and habitat types across North America.

Bighorn sheep are often characterized as grazers, but such a description is not completely accurate. They browse extensively in some habitats and exhibit more flexibility in their diet than many observers realize. Desert bighorns, for example, obtain more of their annual nutritional intake from browsing than grazing in many places. Mountain-mahogany, brittlebush, false mesquite, desert holly, and ironwood are among the woody species browsed by desert bighorns. They are also known to eat saguaro, a treelike cactus native to the Sonoran Desert of southeastern California and southwestern Arizona. Bighorns sometimes feed on the flesh of saguaro, in part to obtain its moisture in the absence of other water sources. In an odd twist of fate, a desert bighorn ewe was once observed with a spine from a saguaro penetrating her lacrimal bone (a small bone found between the eyes), causing

Bighorns are very flexible in their diet. This ewe is grazing on grass near the Colorado River in Grand Canyon National Park. When grass is unavailable, desert bighorns readily turn to browse and may even eat cactus. LISA BALLARD

her blindness and eventual death. The sheep had apparently contacted the spine in an inadvertent collision with a cactus. Desert bighorns are also known to eat prickly pear, barrel cactus, and pincushion cactus.

Bighorns in northern climates consume an eclectic diet, whose composition varies considerably by location and forage availability. Researchers have found that the bighorn sheep ranging from California to British Columbia consume over 260 different species of plants. Rocky Mountain bighorns show a preference for forbs (flowering plants with leaves and stems whose growth dies back to ground level at the end of the growing season). Of the 260-plus plants referenced above, 160 of them are forbs.

The diet of the typical bighorn is composed of grasses, forbs, and shrubs, with the relative percentage of each varying substantially by region. Research on bighorn sheep in Colorado indicates grasses compose 76 percent of their diet, with forbs accounting for 7 percent and shrubs 17 percent. The diet of Montana bighorns was found to be 41 percent grasses, 40 percent forbs, and 19 percent shrubs. Bighorns in California consumed 63 percent forbs and 37 percent grasses. It should be noted that these figures are statewide averages. Bighorns in various regions of states as large as California and Montana may exhibit considerable diversity in their typical diets.

Grasses commonly consumed by bighorns include various types of bluegrass, wheatgrass, fescues, and bromes. Forbs are represented by clovers, phlox, buckwheats, aster, lupine, balsamroot, and paintbrush, among many others. Shrubs often browsed by bighorns consist of chokecherry, several species of sagebrush, mountain mahogany, rabbitbrush, and bitterbrush.

Forage through the Seasons

The diet of bighorn sheep changes with the seasons, sometimes dramatically in relation to the relative percentage of grasses, forbs, and shrubs. Northern-dwelling populations of Rocky Mountain bighorn sheep experience seasonal variations in forage availability most profoundly affected by cold winters and their influence on the plant growth cycle. Seasonal availability of various forage types for desert bighorns is strongly influenced by rainfall. Unusually low annual precipitation or extended drought may alter plant growth and availability for bighorns no matter where they are found.

In the mountainous regions of the Rocky Mountains, forage selection by bighorn sheep follows a somewhat predictable pattern. Forbs are most abundant during the spring and summer, and are most highly represented in the diet of sheep during those seasons. Once they dry and decay in the fall, forbs offer little food value for bighorns.

Shrubs are an important source of nutrition for some bighorns. This ram is browsing on sagebrush in Yellowstone National Park. Browse consumption increases during the winter in some sheep herds. LISA BALLARD

For many Rocky Mountain bighorn sheep herds, grasses are a year-round source of forage. The first green shoots are eagerly consumed in the spring, as are maturing grasses during the summer. Seed-heads and cured grasses are eaten in the fall. Some species of grass experience a fall "green-up" if rain comes after they become dormant and temperatures are warm, providing a windfall of green forage to bighorns and other grazing animals. Dry grasses retain some food value during the winter months and are readily eaten by bighorns. Shrubs are most often consumed during the winter when forbs have become decadent and grasses may be covered in snow.

FORAGE AND FIRE

In the past several decades, wildlife managers have gained a much greater appreciation for the role of wildfires in the creation and maintenance of quality wildlife habitat. While a fire may destroy thousands of acres of forage, the long-term effects of burns, especially on wildlife winter range, are favorable. Many of the forbs relished by bighorns sprout profusely after fire activity, providing an excellent source of spring nutrition. Fires also stimulate grass growth and increase the amount of grass available to bighorns by removing conifer stands on winter range that provide little benefit to wintering sheep.

While the above also benefit other ungulate species, fire may have another positive aspect more specifically related to bighorns. Fires that remove conifers or burn through dense stands of timber broaden the visual horizon, making such areas more suitable to bighorns who seldom venture into heavy cover. I have personally observed bighorns grazing in a burned area that five years previously was covered with a fairly dense stand of lodgepole pines. Research in Idaho and British Columbia has shown bighorns using burned areas more heavily than adjacent unburned habitat for at least four years following the fire.

With the above factors in mind, biologists are currently reevaluating fire-suppression practices in wildlife habitat. In some areas fires are deliberately set under controlled conditions to improve bighorn sheep habitat, primarily on winter range. While forest fires that destroy homes or other property are certainly a cause for alarm, flames in wildlife habitat unoccupied by humans are usually good for a wide range of animals.

Forest fires open timber and rejuvenate forage for bighorns. This previously burned area in Colorado provides potential forage for sheep and other wildlife. SHUTTERSTOCK

Migration

Bighorn sheep migrations are usually associated with seasonal changes in the elevation at which animals are found in an ecosystem. Mountain-dwelling populations of bighorn sheep typically spend their summers in the alpine zone at very high elevations. Research on the nutritional value of grass species has compared high-elevation grasses with those growing in the foothills. Even within the same species, nutritional value is higher for plants found at lofty elevations. Many experts believe the availability of forage with superior nutritional value is what leads bighorns to their alpine haunts in the summer.

Increasing snow depth and cold temperatures are conditions thought to be instrumental in triggering the migration of bighorns from the highlands to winter range at lower elevations or in the foothills. The trek to winter range in most populations of Rocky Mountain bighorns occurs in October and November.

Fall migrations from alpine environments to mountain foothills are common among bighorns. This small band was photographed in the foothills of the Absaroka Mountains in Montana in November after migrating from summer habitat on the mountaintops.

Rocky Mountain bighorns that spend the entire year at high elevation may move from one alpine area to another, diverse habitat niches that represent distinct summer and winter ranges. Females complete the fall migration before males. The spring return to higher pastures happens as early as April or as late as July, depending on the area and seasonal conditions. Bighorns tend to follow greening forage up the mountains, a phenomenon that may be accelerated or retarded by snow depth and temperature. A discernible pattern of spring migration between the sexes is not apparent.

Some desert bighorns also engage in migrations. These may be seasonal movements between various mountain ranges

Desert bighorn sheep sometimes engage in migrations that allow them to utilize the best portions of habitat within their range at various times of the year or in response to changing forage conditions. SHUTTERSTOCK

covering considerable distances, or elevation-related migrations occurring within a particular mountain range. Seasonal availability of water sources may also trigger migrations of desert bighorns. Like the migrations of Rocky Mountain bighorns, recurring movements of desert animals appear to be prompted by a motivation to exploit the most desirable swatches of habitat within a sheep's range.

CHAPTER 4 Abilities and Behavior

Physical Abilities

The physical traits of wild hoofed mammals are remarkably adapted to the habitats in which they live, including specialized abilities that help them escape predators. Pronghorn are exceptionally fleet of foot, so fast that no predator on the North American continent can match their speed in a chase. Moose have excellent hearing and can trot at high speeds through forests and over obstacles, which makes it difficult for would-be predators to catch them.

Bighorn sheep have neither the speed of the pronghorn nor the hearing of a moose. Nonetheless, they are extremely adept at eluding predators in the steep, rocky places they inhabit. The muscles on the hindquarters of a bighorn sheep are very

Strong muscles in the rear quarters give bighorns the power to make incredible leaps in steep terrain. SHUTTERSTOCK

developed. These muscles propel them in powerful leaps that may take them from ledge to ledge on a vertical rock face or in a quick dash from a grassy area to a jumble of stones. The relatively short, blocky bodies of bighorns aren't built for speed in the open country. Some historical accounts indicate bighorns caught in the open could be easily overtaken by a pack of dogs or run down by a rider on horseback. However, when it comes to running up or down steep slopes, bighorns are very fast and agile.

The ability of bighorns to traverse seemingly impossible terrain is legendary. They are sometimes observed on cliff ledges or rocky promontories where it seems impossible to stand. However, bighorns have several physical adaptations that permit such abilities. First, their bodies are very strong and compact, allowing them to brace against the forces of gravity and maneuver in places creatures with larger limbs or bodies find it impossible to follow. Bighorns also possess hooves that lend them extremely

Specialized hooves and spectacular balance allow bighorn sheep to traverse cliffs where predators are unable to follow. SHUTTERSTOCK

Eyesight is the sense bighorns rely upon most heavily to detect predators. This ewe from Yellowstone National Park, Wyoming, can see movement of small objects at a distance of 1,000 yards. LISA BALLARD

efficient gripping ability on slick or steep rocks. The cloven hooves of bighorns consist of two digits that can move independently of each other. A spongy portion is found on the rear of each part of the hoof with a rubbery outer covering, yielding a substance that provides the bighorn with outstanding traction on hard, slippery surfaces. The front hooves of bighorns are slightly larger than the rear hooves, a characteristic thought to aid their exceptional climbing ability. Although bighorn sheep sometimes slip and fall from cliffs, occasionally sustaining serious or fatal injuries, these occurrences appear to be quite rare, indicating bighorns also possess an uncanny sense of balance and precision of movement in constrained space.

Of their perceptive organs, bighorns appear to rely on their eyes more than other senses to detect other animals, including predators. Some sources claim the eyesight of bighorn sheep is approximately eight times better than that of humans. Such claims, though common in relation to the vision of animals, are seldom scientifically tested. The ability of bighorns to discern motion at considerable distances has been documented, but definitive studies of their perceptual abilities are lacking. Bighorns can detect the movement of other creatures at a distance of 1,000 yards. The keen eyesight of bighorn sheep is also thought to be instrumental in the animals' prowess in jumping and perceiving footholds in perilous terrain.

Animals inhabiting dense, forested habitats, both predators and prey, often display exceptional hearing and sense of smell. These abilities allow them to discern other creatures where eyesight is impeded. The ears of bighorn sheep are quite small compared to those of elk, mule, or whitetail deer. While bighorns can probably detect sound as well as humans, their hearing is not nearly as developed as deer or elk. It is interesting to note that the other animal that shares the bighorn's affinity for cliffs and steep places, the mountain goat, also has small ears in relation to its size. The same holds true for the bighorn sheep's sense of smell. Bighorns sometimes detect predators via their nose, and rams have been observed following unseen ewes on the basis of scent. However, in the world of North American ungulates, the bighorn's sense of smell appears to be inferior to many of its kin.

One of the most remarkable physical abilities of bighorn sheep is their endurance of extremely cold temperatures. Bighorns wintering on high alpine ridges may encounter temperatures below 0°F for extended periods of time. How do they keep from freezing to death? Research has found that the bodies of bighorn sheep are extremely efficient at producing and retaining heat. At around 10°F bighorns achieve a state of thermal neutrality. "Thermal-neutral" is a term used to describe the temperature at which an organism doesn't burn energy to stay warm or cool itself. The compact body of bighorns, an efficient metabolism, and a super-insulating coat are among the adaptations allowing sheep to thrive in low temperatures. However, when temperatures increase in the summer, bighorns spend considerable energy keeping their bodies cool. Desert bighorns seek out shade in caves or under trees to stay cool. Rocky Mountain bighorns move to high elevations to find forage, but may also be motivated

Bighorns have an amazing ability to endure cold. Metabolic adaptations and a super-insulating coat allow them to conserve energy throughout the winter.

by the cooler temperatures. The circulatory system becomes more active in higher temperatures to help the animals disperse heat.

Vocal and Visual Communication

Bighorn sheep, like other herd animals, frequently use vocalizations as a means of communication. Ewes and lambs often communicate with bleats that sound similar to the "baah, baah" noises made by domestic sheep. Newborn lambs and their mothers bleat back and forth frequently after birth, apparently to strengthen the mother-offspring bond and to familiarize each other with their voice. When the ewe needs to find her lamb within the maternal herd (or vice versa), she will not only look for her young but also bleat to get its attention. Once found, the mother sniffs the youngster, in what appears to be a behavior that confirms its identity.

Research has indicated that young lambs rely more on sound to identify their mothers than sight or smell. Although ewes and lambs become attuned to each other's voices, the vocal means of identification isn't perfect. Occasionally ewes will respond to the bleats of a lamb in the herd that is not her own. However, the unique smell of the offspring is a more accurate way to recognize

HUMAN TOLERATION

As human population in the United States continues to grow and dwellings are constructed in desirable locations in the Rocky Mountains, bighorn sheep are increasingly exposed to people. In most cases a general wariness in the presence of predators is considered a survival advantage among prey species such as bighorns. However, in today's world sheep with higher toleration levels for humans may be better equipped to thrive than those who prefer to keep their distance.

Real estate development on winter range and outdoor recreation activities such as hiking, mountain biking, and

In an ever-changing world, bighorns that develop a toleration of humans may be better equipped to survive than their more "wild" brethren.

cross-country skiing bring people into bighorn habitat. Individual sheep with a higher toleration for people may be less likely to be displaced from prime habitat and exert less effort to move away from people, thereby increasing their access to good forage and conserving energy reserves in the winter, two factors that potentially give them a survival advantage over their more skittish counterparts.

Ideally people will voluntarily give bighorns (and other wildlife) the space they need to live in peace. In areas where this doesn't happen, animals with a "tame" disposition may have a stronger chance of maintaining their species than those that are "wild."

Rams use many sophisticated means of physical communication. Older rams may rest their head on the back of a younger male in a display of dominance.

its individuality. Ewes will not accept a lamb that fails to pass the scent test.

One of the loudest and dramatic noises created by bighorn sheep is not used as a means of communication. During the mating season, rams clash their horns together in battles for dominance. The sharp cracking sounds made when the rams butt their heads together can sometimes be heard at a distance of a mile, and may alert a person of the presence of bighorn rams.

Like other mother-offspring pairs in the world of ungulates, bighorn ewes and lambs communicate their bond with physical behaviors as well as vocalizations. They many nuzzle one another, or the mother may butt a pesky offspring or another lamb. However, perhaps the most complex and interesting forms of physical communication occur between adult rams. Throughout the year, rams assert or accept dominance of other males. Subordinate rams nuzzle their superiors. They may wag their horns at rams of equal or higher social status in a gesture that suggests submission, not a challenge. Dominant rams may place their head on the neck or back of a subordinate, or mount them from behind. To initiate a challenge to a dominant ram, an upstart subordinate may kick its belly to incite a confrontation.

Herd Behavior

Bighorn sheep may sometimes be found alone, particularly yearlings or old rams, but the vast majority live in herds whose composition shifts at various times during the year. Except during the mating season, older rams live in bands separately from ewes and lambs.

Juvenile rams stay in female bands composed of adult ewes and their offspring for up to three years, rarely beyond. Some research suggests young rams transition from female herds to groups of adult males when they become dominant animals in the female bands. Studies of bighorns in some locations also suggest young rams join herds of adult males as they travel to mineral licks, places where sheep deliberately ingest soil to obtain minerals that apparently enhance their health. The number of individuals in a herd of rams varies significantly in relation to habitat and the number of bighorns occupying a particular region. Ram bands may consist of just two or three individuals, or may hold over a dozen adult rams of different ages.

Except during the mating season, mature rams are usually found in "bachelor herds" that contain only males. SHUTTERSTOCK

Female herds of bighorn sheep normally live in different places than the ram bands, except during the mating season when the separate groups intermingle. Like ram bands, the size of female herds varies dramatically, depending on habitat and sheep population in a given area. One interesting variation in female herds occurs when pregnant ewes depart the female bands to birth their young. At these times sheep may congregate in female herds led by barren ewes, often older animals beyond prime reproductive age. The barren ewes are accompanied by immature rams and yearlings of both sexes separated from their mothers for the first time. Young sheep that haven't learned independent living strategies greatly benefit from their association with these matriarchs as they transition to adulthood, and enjoy greater survival rates than immature sheep forced to live on their own.

CHAPTER 5 Reproduction and Young

The Mating Season

The mating season, or "rut," for mammal species is understood by biologists as the period of time in which reproductive behaviors between males and females result in a large percentage of the offspring crop for a given season. As is the case with numerous other mammal species, the mating season for bighorn sheep in northern latitudes and high elevations is more circumscribed than those living in milder climates. The reason for this is simple: Offspring born on either side of an optimal period in cold climates have a substantially reduced chance of survival. For example, a bighorn lamb birthed too early in the spring in the northern

The mating season for desert bighorns, like this pair in Arizona, is much longer than for bighorns in northern climates. SHUTTERSTOCK

Rocky Mountains may freeze to death in a late-arriving storm. Lambs whose birthdays occur in midsummer may initially benefit from warmer temperature and the presence of succulent forage. However, late-born bighorns are smaller and less vigorous entering their first winter than older offspring, reducing their odds of surviving to their first birthday.

In contrast, lambs born in warmer climates aren't at risk of freezing in a late storm or required to endure frigid temperatures or forced to navigate snowy terrain in their first winter. Thus, the mating (and birthing) season for desert bighorn sheep is much longer and less intense than for Rocky Mountain bighorns inhabiting northern portions of their range. Researchers have documented the birth of desert bighorns in various parts of their range on nearly a year-round basis. For example, bighorns in the Sonoran Desert of Arizona are known to have produced lambs in every month of the year except October. Some other desert bighorn sheep populations have mating and birthing seasons that are more circumscribed. Rocky Mountain bighorns in Canada and the northern United States typically mate in November and December, with some populations beginning the rut in mid-November and breeding activity persisting into mid-January.

Competition among rams for females represents one of the most dramatic seasons in the annual life-cycle of bighorn sheep. Males whose rivalry can't be resolved with dominance displays or intimidation settle their differences head-to-head. Rams battle by head-butting. Rival males clash their horns and skulls together in fierce butting bouts that may last for many hours. The most forcible battles involve fights that see two rams rearing at a distance of 10 yards or more, then lunging toward one another at speeds of 20 miles per hour. The force of the impact between battering rams is sufficient to crush and kill a human. Rams possess specialized skulls and muscular-skeletal structures in their necks that allow them to absorb such violent contact. However, the fights do sometimes result in serious injuries such as broken jaws or noses and eye trauma. The horns of adult rams often bear the marks

Rams clash horns in battles to determine dominance. These equally matched rams were photographed fighting in Custer State Park, South Dakota. LISA BALLARD

Ewes, like this one being guarded from other males by a mature ram in Yellowstone National Park, actively seek the attention of large males. SHUTTERSTOCK

SIZE MATTERS

Rams may become fertile before they reach one year of age in the desert bighorn subspecies. Research indicates Rocky Mountain rams become capable of reproduction a bit later, but may attain such status by eighteen months of age. However, in most populations rams do not reproduce until much later. Observations of Rocky Mountain bighorns show that in most populations rams will not play a major role in reproduction until their seventh or eighth year.

By this time males on good range will have attained both body weight and horn mass greatly superior to young rams. They are able to dominate immature males and are more readily accepted by breeding females.

Although younger rams can successfully impregnate ewes, in both captive and wild populations, the presence of massive, monarch rams plays a role in the health of sheep herds beyond reproduction. Young rams tend to be aggressive and overly energetic in their pursuit of females on the breeding grounds, not only depleting their own energy reserves but those of the ewes fleeing their untimely advances. Older rams, by contrast, are more reserved in their courtship. Their intolerance of young

of battle, including chipping and damage to the horn bases and splintered tips.

Contrary to some accounts of bighorn sheep natural history, the dominance battles of rams do not normally occur during the mating season, but before it. The pecking order among rams is established in bachelor groups before they join the ewe herds on mating grounds. During the rut, mature rams spend their time courting and repelling younger rams from females. Sexually mature but subordinate rams may expend considerable effort to chase a receptive ewe from the presence of a dominant ram.

The presence of large, heavy-horned rams improves the overall health and reproduction of bighorn sheep herds. SHUTTERSTOCK

males creates a buffer between ewes and immature rams that allows ewes to conceive offspring without wasting energy and depleting body reserves running from inexperienced rams.

When it comes to the health of a bighorn herd, the presence of a few monarch rams is better than a dozen lesser males. Size matters.

Although it is assumed by some observers that rams play the central role during the rut, observations by researchers have shown that ewes are selective in the breeding process, actively seeking the attention of rams on the mating grounds with the largest bodies and horns.

Pregnancy and Gestation

Research with captive bighorn sheep has shown that the period of time between the initiation of pregnancy and birth (gestation period) is around 175 days, over three weeks longer than the gestation period of domestic sheep. The reproduction efficiency of bighorn sheep females is highly correlated to body weight and forage availability and quality. Age also plays a role in reproduction. Ewes in Rocky Mountain populations typically bear their first offspring at three years of age, although some may reproduce as two-year-olds in expanding populations or under unusual circumstances. Desert bighorns are sometimes reproductive at younger ages than their Rocky Mountain counterparts. Researchers have observed yearling ewes with lambs in California and Nevada. Elderly ewes rarely breed and produce young.

Pregnancy rates among fertile bighorn sheep females are very high. Desert bighorn ewes typically conceive lambs at a rate of around 75 percent to 85 percent depending on the population. Among Rocky Mountain bighorns the conception rates are even higher. It is not unusual for females in local herds of the northern-dwelling subspecies to experience conception rates of 90 percent.

Birth

Lambs are usually born in May and June in most populations of Rocky Mountain bighorns. However, later births are known to occur in some herds occupying high-elevation habitat. Some lambs are born earlier in southern populations of the Rocky Mountain subspecies. April births have been documented in California and may happen elsewhere in southern ranges. The offspring of desert bighorns may be born at almost any time of the year, depending on the patterns of local animals. However, the typical birthing season is often reported as occurring between December and June, with most births taking place between February and May.

Bighorn sheep normally birth a single offspring. Twins have been documented, but the occurrence of multiple offspring is extremely low and is not considered to be a significant factor in reproduction rates or herd growth.

Prior to birthing their lambs, ewes retreat to rugged areas, most often among cliffs or exceedingly steep terrain. In northwestern Wyoming I have observed bighorn ewes with tiny lambs

Bighorn sheep normally birth a single lamb. Twins, like these born to a radio-collared ewe in Badlands National Park, South Dakota, are quite rare. SHUTTERSTOCK

Bighorn ewes use cliffs and rocky terrain where lambs are buffered from predation as birthing sites. SHUTTERSTOCK

inhabiting navigable terrain between two sheer cliff faces. Protection from predators that mark lambs as easy prey is assumed to be the primary reason ewes birth their offspring in such places, but climate may play a role as well. In northern latitudes very steep, south-facing slopes afford baby bighorns increased exposure to sunlight, which may result in warmer surroundings and better survival in colder-than-average temperatures. Birthing sites may be used by individual ewes or females in a particular herd on a year-after-year basis.

The actual birthing process of wild bighorn sheep is seldom witnessed, but research with captive animals indicates actual labor is brief, averaging less than twenty minutes. Prior to labor, bighorn ewes show signs of the impending birth, including pacing and sometimes pawing at the earth. Newborn lambs usually stand and nurse very quickly, with most lambs starting their first nursing within an hour of birth. Lambs that receive frequent attention from their mothers, such as nuzzling or licking, stand and nurse earlier than those born to less-attentive females. Baby bighorns normally walk within the first hour or two of being born.

Rocky Mountain bighorn lambs typically weigh between 6.2 and 12 pounds. Desert bighorn babies are usually a bit smaller, with an average birth weight of about 6.4 pounds. Differences in birth weights related to the sex of the offspring are insignificant.

Nurturing Lambs to Adulthood

Although bighorn sheep exhibit high conception and birth rates, mortality among young sheep is very high. Occasionally as few as 5 percent of the lambs born within an area will survive to see their first birthday, especially among herds subject to disease or extreme weather conditions. Even among relatively healthy desert bighorns, first-year survival rates as low as 20 percent are not unusual.

A number of hazards account for deaths among young bighorns. Survival in the first year is profoundly influenced by weather events. Very young lambs born in alpine environments are susceptible to hypothermia (decreased body temperature caused

Athletic and playful, bighorn lambs grow quickly. They face many survival challenges in their first year of life. SHUTTERSTOCK

by cold, wind, precipitation, or some combination thereof). It is not well known if hypothermia is a direct cause of death among bighorn lambs. However, the weakening effects of the condition are believed by many biologists to be instrumental in a decreased resistance to illness and impaired growth, both of which diminish a young sheep's prospects of survival.

The offspring of desert bighorns can be stricken when drought leaves its mother with too little forage for milk production, leading to malnutrition. Biologists theorize that in some cases young desert bighorns may be at risk when precipitation levels are much higher than average as well. Excess groundwater in the form of ponds and pools may spawn swarms of biting insects carrying fatal diseases.

In some areas significant numbers of young bighorns are killed in the first few months of life by predators, a topic we'll explore more fully in chapter 6. However, the dramatic and devastating effects of respiratory disease appear to be the number one factor that limits lamb survival and bighorn sheep numbers.

Bighorn lambs grow rapidly. By six months of age, many desert bighorns will weigh ten times more than their birth weight. Birth weight and subsequent weight gain are extremely important for survival in the first year of a bighorn's life. Research indicates lambs with lower birth weights have lower survival rates than their heavier counterparts. Lambs that fail to grow adequately may die directly from starvation or secondary issues related to malnutrition. Larger young with superior body condition are better prepared to endure the rigors of their first winter among northern populations. At one year of age, rams are noticeably bigger than ewes. Reported average yearling weights for the sexes in desert bighorns are 122 pounds for rams and 100 pounds for ewes.

In their second year, bighorn sheep face another survival challenge. Yearlings are separated from their mother when she prepares to birth the next year's lamb. Those that attach themselves to older, barren females have a leader to follow. Yearlings forced to live on their own may wander into habitats unfit for bighorns or areas where they are easily targeted by predators.

At around two years of age, the growth histories of rams and ewes diverge. Females reach their adult weight at around three or four years, but males continue to grow until age six or beyond. Researchers have recorded weight differences between the sexes in bighorns favoring rams by 18 percent at age two, 65 percent at age six. Among desert bighorns, survival rates increase dramatically once a sheep reaches two years, then begin to decrease at age seven.

CHAPTER 6 Bighorn Sheep and Other Animals

Bighorns and Other Ungulates

Bighorn sheep share their range with a considerable number of other ungulates in various habitats throughout North America. Desert bighorns, for example, live in places uninhabitable to moose. Rocky Mountain bighorns in mountainous areas in states

Elk consume many of the same food sources as bighorns. Some biologists theorize that an abundance of elk on winter range might negatively affect sheep, but research on the relationship between the two animals is lacking. SHUTTERSTOCK

such as Montana, Wyoming, and Idaho may occasionally cross paths with moose. Bighorns in prairie habitats including eastern Montana, North Dakota, and South Dakota may find themselves in proximity to pronghorn, while sheep dwelling in mountainous regions do not. Prairie and mountain herds of bighorns come into contact with mule deer. Both Rocky Mountain and desert bighorns are frequently found on the same range as mule deer. Sheep wintering in foothills locations in the Rockies can sometimes be seen in proximity to elk, and less frequently come into contact with whitetail deer.

Direct interactions between bighorns and the ungulate species noted above are probably uncommon and infrequently observed by humans. Biologists are generally unconcerned with the impact these ungulates might have on bighorns. One exception might concern utilization of winter range. In the case of elk, both bighorns and elk are generalist feeders that consume both grasses and browse in the winter. It seems reasonable to assume high numbers of elk on winter range might decrease the amount of forage available for bighorns, but research addressing this relationship is lacking.

Bighorn sheep share summer and winter range with mountain goats in many areas in the northern Rocky Mountains. In some places, such as Montana's Glacier National Park, bighorns and goats have tracked the same crags and alpine meadows for thousands of years. Elsewhere, native bighorns have come into contact with transplanted mountain goats in fairly recent times. Introduced, nonnative populations of mountain goats now share habitat with bighorn sheep in portions of Idaho, Montana, Wyoming, Nevada, Utah, and Colorado. Expansion of mountain goat range in those areas has brought increasing numbers of bighorns into contact with nonnative mountain goats.

Although it's well known that mountain goats and bighorn sheep can and do coexist without apparent harm to either species, the introduced populations of mountain goats in the above states are of concern to many biologists involved in bighorn sheep management and research.

In the era when goats hit the ground in Montana, Colorado, and Idaho, the desirability of relocating animals to establish populations for hunting provided the impetus for the transplants. Little thought appears to have been given to the broader questions of the animals' impact on native ecosystems, including the other mammals with which the newcomers would interact. Such was the case with mountain goats.

From a wildlife management perspective, two issues have emerged in relation to transplanted mountain goats and bighorn sheep. The first has to do with habitat. In the extreme environments the two species occupy, palatable forage is sometimes at

Nonnative mountain goats may transmit diseases to native bighorn sheep. The ancestors of these goats in Yellowstone National Park arrived there via transplants in Montana.
SHUTTERSTOCK

NONNATIVES IN NATIONAL PARKS

The presence of nonnative mountain goats and their potential to compete with native bighorn sheep for forage or to transmit disease is becoming a thorny issue in several national parks. In 1997 President Jimmy Carter signed Executive Order #11987, which restricted the introduction of nonnative species on federal lands. The order has been largely ineffectual, but the National Park Service (NPS) is one of the federal agencies that has developed policies that prioritize the health and preservation of native species over nonnatives. Thus, fisheries management in places like Yellowstone and Grand Teton National Parks favors endemic cutthroat trout over introduced rainbow trout.

If NPS policy frowns upon the presence of nonnative wildlife, even species inhabiting similar habitats in other parts of the United States, the presence of mountain goats in several national parks is a cause for concern. Indeed, from November to December 2013, the NPS conducted a scoping period for the development of an environmental assessment to determine how to handle the colonizing mountain goats in Grand Teton National Park. Grand Teton isn't the only national park where biologists are warily watching a growing goat presence. Yellowstone shares the issue, along with Colorado's Rocky Mountain National Park. Olympic National Park in Washington is also home to nonnative goats, and a hiker was killed by an aggressive goat there in 2010.

Like many other nonnative species that have become naturalized in an area, mountain goats in national parks are regarded as native creatures by many observers who relish the sighting of one. Most hikers in the Tetons, for example, are happy to report the presence of goats. Should the NPS move to eliminate mountain goats from national parks, a certain amount of public backlash is the most predictable result. Additionally, eradicating goats from parks is probably not feasible. If the present population is removed, others will almost certainly recolonize from outside, and it's not like a goat-proof barbwire fence can be constructed around an entire national park to keep them out.

However, the NPS policy that prohibits the introduction of nonnative species and prioritizes the preservation of natives recognizes a simple but far-reaching biological principle. Nonnative plants and animals are often detrimental to indigenous species, sometimes through interactions that take decades to document and determine. Mountain goats and bighorn sheep have coexisted in Glacier National Park, Montana, for centuries. How transplanted goats may affect bighorns in other national parks remains to be seen.

Bighorns and mountain goats have coexisted in Glacier National Park (where the image of this ram was taken) for centuries. SHUTTERSTOCK

a minimum. Will a herd of fifty mountain goats reduce the feed available to bighorn sheep, particularly at times of the year or in habitat niches where sheep are most vulnerable?

It is disease, however, not forage or competition for other valuable habitat commodities like secure birthing sites, that is of greatest concern to many state and federal biologists observing the growing and expanding mountain goat presence in bighorn sheep habitat. Bighorn sheep are notoriously susceptible to diseases, especially pneumonia. Disease transmission from domestic sheep to bighorns is invariably disastrous. Is it possible that colonizing mountain goats are also carrying diseases to bighorns?

In fact, biologists and wildlife disease specialists in Wyoming have concluded that mountain goats carry all of the pathogens that are potentially lethal to bighorns. Even though researchers haven't tested as many goats as sheep, research indicates goats are capable of carrying and spreading pathogens to sheep. Most biologists aren't particularly concerned about goats causing catastrophic collapses in sheep herds. For the most part, it appears bighorns currently sharing range with mountain goats already carry some mix of the pneumonia-causing bugs so fatal to bighorns under certain conditions. However, if goats continue to expand into other mountain ranges, they may eventually come into contact with sheep herds that are disease-free. If the ranges of goats or sheep change, the disease issue may become much more problematic.

Bighorns and Predators

Living among cliffs and badland environments give the powerful, agile bighorn sheep an effective means of escaping predators. Nonetheless, a wide array of predators have the ability to prey upon bighorns, though few predators routinely target sheep as prey. Among those, mountain lions (cougars) and coyotes may be the most potent predators. Mountain lions are capable of killing adult bighorns of both genders. Mountain lion predation has been recorded virtually everywhere the two species coexist.

Mountain lions are perhaps the only predator in North America capable of consistently preying upon adult bighorn sheep. Predation by mountain lions has impeded bighorn transplant projects in several southwestern states. SHUTTERSTOCK

The killing of bighorns by cougars appears to be a significant factor in the establishment and maintenance of desert bighorn herds in a number of areas. Desert bighorn introductions in New Mexico, Utah, Texas, and Arizona have been abandoned or severely hampered by mountain lion predation. Biologists theorize that introduced populations may be particularly susceptible to predation by the big cats until sheep discover and learn to use preferable escape terrain. In California, mountain lion predation is considered to be an impediment to the recovery of the endangered Sierra Nevada bighorn sheep in and around Yosemite National Park.

Mountain lion predation on bighorn sheep is a complex phenomenon. Research on the relationship is sparse, but two factors appear to increase predation on sheep by these formidable feline predators. First, predation on bighorns by mountain lions is thought to be most acute where sheep share range with mule deer. Mule deer are a primary prey species for mountain lions in many regions. In such places bighorns may become frequent targets of cougar predation if mule deer numbers are depressed or at times of the year (primarily winter and early spring) when sheep are more vulnerable to predation. A second important factor involves prey specialization by mountain lions. Within a cougar population, certain cats may focus on particular species of prey. Such is seemingly the case with bighorns. In most areas where mountain lions prey on substantial numbers of sheep, it is relatively few of the cougars that do most of the killing.

Coyotes, like mountain lions, take considerable numbers of bighorn sheep in some areas. Lambs are most vulnerable to coyote predation. In British Columbia, researchers have documented predation rates by coyotes as high as 80 percent on lambs in the first year of life. Some biologists theorize that coyote predation is higher in places lacking adequate escape terrain, most notably in areas where bighorns have been introduced outside their native range. Coyote packs are also capable of killing adult bighorns, although coyote predation on adult sheep is not considered a principle source of mortality.

A number of other mammalian species are either known or assumed predators of bighorn sheep, though none are thought to exert any instrumental effect on bighorn numbers. These

Golden eagles prey upon bighorn lambs in a variety of habitats. Ewes are frequently successful in repelling the attacks of eagles against their lambs.

include black and grizzly bears, wolves, wolverines, lynx, bobcats, jaguars, ocelots, and some species of foxes. Evidence of predation or actual predation on bighorns by most of these species has been infrequently observed.

A final bighorn sheep predator worthy of note has feathers, not fangs. Golden eagles are known to be regular predators of bighorn lambs in some places, although they take relatively few young. Eagles may be capable of killing older sheep in certain circumstances. Some observational evidence suggests golden eagle predation becomes more acute after severe winters when these imposing raptors have fewer prey choices. Eyewitness accounts have shown that bighorn ewes will actively defend their young against eagles or sometimes take them into heavier cover when eagles are present, one of the few instances in which bighorns will deliberately choose denser vegetation over more open slopes.

Parasites and Diseases

In appearance and in relation to the demanding habitats they frequent, bighorn sheep might easily be assumed as one of the toughest mammalian species on the planet. When it comes to diseases, nothing could be further from the truth. Entire herds of a hundred or more animals may be decimated by disease in less than a year in epidemics killing 80 percent or more of the animals in a short period of time. Many herds never recover from the maladies and eventually become extinct.

Pneumonia is the disease most often associated with plague-like decimation of bighorn sheep herds. At the present time, wildlife disease specialists have implicated several strains of bacteria in widespread bighorn die-offs associated with the disease. However, the specific pathology of pneumonia in bighorns is poorly understood. Healthy bighorns can carry the pathogens that spawn pneumonia for years without appearing or acting sick. Some wildlife disease specialists believe some combination of stress, nutritional deprivation, and invasion by various pathogens trigger disastrous pneumonia outbreaks in herds already carrying pathogens. During the 2009–10 winter, dramatic pneumonia epidemics afflicted bighorn sheep herds in four states (Montana, Nevada, Washington, and Utah). The disease events caused from 33 to 95 percent die-offs among bighorns. Lamb survival is typically low in herds experiencing pneumonia outbreaks for three to ten years after the event, making population recoveries very slow. In many cases bighorn sheep herds never recover to previous levels after a pneumonia epidemic.

Contact with domestic sheep is often the cause for pneumonia in bighorns. Domestic sheep have evolved to harbor the pathogens that cause pneumonia in bighorns without harm to themselves. The abundance of bighorn sheep in the contiguous United States prior to European settlement, and their inability to recover to the extent of other species such as elk and bison, gives some indication of the degree to which contact with domestic livestock makes them vulnerable to disease. Reducing contact between bighorns and domestic sheep is considered by biologists to be essential to the survival of the *Ovis canadensis* species.

Along with pneumonia, diseases common to other ungulates also afflict bighorn sheep. Bighorns may contract paratuberculosis (Johne's disease), contagious ecthyma (sore mouth), bluetongue, chronic sinusitis, and mandibular osteomyelitis (lumpy jaw). These diseases are not believed to be instrumental in suppressing bighorn sheep populations, but may intermittently inhibit production in some areas. Capture myopathy, a syndrome brought about by extreme stress or exercise and sometimes associated with trapping of bighorns for transplantation or research purposes, is also sometimes listed among bighorn sheep diseases. The condition affects bodily systems of bighorn sheep in sudden, disruptive ways that may lead to severe shock and death. Capture myopathy appears in other ungulate species including elk, deer, antelope, moose, and mountain goats. Minimization of stress during handling and the appropriate administration of immobilizing drugs greatly reduce the possibility of animals succumbing to the condition.

Ungulates in North America are often hosts to a broad range of external and internal parasites. Bighorn sheep are buffered from certain parasites due to the harsh environments they inhabit but nonetheless may be inflicted with dozens of parasites. Ticks, fleas, biting midges, and other external parasites may cause discomfort to sheep, but are little threat to the welfare of healthy

The picture of health and vigor, a pneumonia outbreak can strike bighorns like this ram in a matter of weeks.

bighorns receiving adequate nutrition. A variety of internal parasites, including intestinal worms and flukes (many of them introduced to wild populations of ungulates via livestock), are also known to invade bighorn sheep. Little research has been done to determine how these parasites might influence the health of bighorns, but it is assumed that high densities of such parasites might weaken sheep, perhaps making them more vulnerable to winter starvation or predation. One internal parasite, lungworms, are of greater concern. Lungworm infestations in bighorns have been implicated in pneumonia outbreaks and high lamb mortality.

CHAPTER 7 Bighorn Sheep and Humans

Bighorns and American Indians

Images of bighorn sheep painted or etched on rocks are found in numerous locations across the western United States. Created long before the arrival of European settlers, the origins and dates of the rock art are unknown, but are thought by some archaeologists to be at least 3,000 years old. The purpose of the primitive artistic endeavors are a matter of speculation. Some experts believe the images, which are often found in places bighorns lived and could have been hunted, were seen by their makers as good luck charms to ensure the success of sheep hunts. Others feel the representations of sheep had a religious purpose, while some scholars admit they may have been merely artwork, similar to modern drawings with sidewalk chalk or roadside graffiti.

Petroglyphs of bighorn sheep are found in many places in the southwestern United States. Some are thought to be at least 3,000 years old. SHUTTERSTOCK

The horns of bighorn sheep were used by American Indians to create utensils such as spoons. Bows fashioned from rams' horns were very valuable to native peoples. LISA BALLARD

While the role of bighorn sheep in such ancient artwork is unknown, history validates the utilization of bighorns in numerous American Indian cultures. Bighorns were hunted for food and their horns were used in the construction of various implements, such as spoons and bowls. One of the most fascinating connections between bighorn sheep and native peoples of North America involves a clan of Shoshone Indians who inhabited the region in and around Yellowstone National Park prior to European settlement.

The name *"Shoshone"* hearkens to a loosely confederated group of American Indians that is thought to have migrated from the Great Basin area between California and Nevada northward to the Salmon River region of Idaho and northwestern Wyoming. Subgroups of the Shoshone were linguistically classified by their primary diet. The Shoshones included "eaters of pine nuts," "eaters of salmon," and "buffalo eaters." A relatively small group of Shoshones known as the "sheep eaters" inhabited the Greater Yellowstone region. Although their diet also consisted of roots, berries, and other game animals such as elk, this singular people depended heavily on the bighorn sheep for its sustenance. The mountainous ungulates provided meat and clothing.

Sheep-eater artisans also fashioned beautiful bows from the sweeping horns of bighorn rams through a process that possibly involved heating the horns in local hot springs. It took the native craftsmen up to two months to complete the construction of a horn bow. The hunting implements were quite compact, typically measuring just under 3 feet in length, and very strong. Sheep-eater bows were highly prized by other tribes as well. Some historians believe sheep-horn bows had a value similar to that of ten horses in regional trade. While many native tribes readily assimilated the horse and European firearms into their culture and hunting practices, the sheep eaters found little use for them. They relied on pack dogs to carry their possessions, creatures much more suited to travel in rugged mountains than horses, and highly sophisticated hunting methods to kill sheep that didn't require the use of a long-range rifle.

The Crow Indians, native to Montana and Wyoming, revered the bighorn sheep. Little Big Horn College, a two-year tribal college located on the Crow Indian Reservation in Montana, is specifically named in honor of the bighorn sheep in Crow legend. According to the legend, a young Crow boy was cast over a cliff in the Big Horn Mountains (in northern Wyoming) by his stepfather.

Crow Indian legend tells of a leader who was raised by a band of bighorn rams as a boy.
SHUTTERSTOCK

His family assumed him dead, but the youth was saved by seven bighorn rams who raised him to adulthood. Along the way the rams instructed him in the principles of the bighorn's way of life. As an adult, the boy returned to the Crow people and became known as Big Metal. Tribal tradition attributes the wisdom of the people to Big Metal and the seven bighorn rams who mentored him. The mascot of Little Big Horn College is the Ram. Numerous geographical features in Crow country bear the name of their beloved sheep, including the Big Horn Mountains and the Big Horn and Little Big Horn Rivers.

Bighorns and European Settlers

Spanish explorers encountered bighorn sheep in southwestern regions of North America as early as the sixteenth century. Jesuit missionaries in what is now the northern part of Mexico and the southwestern United States were aware of the bighorn prior to 1700. European experience with bighorns in the Rocky Mountains accelerated in the early decades of the nineteenth century with exploration of the region and the increasing forays of fur trappers. Bighorns dwelling in rough country along the rivers of the plains and mountain foothills were sometimes hunted by pioneering trappers and explorers, especially in the winter when found at low elevations. Bighorns occupying mountainous areas were often viewed as quarry whose effort to obtain them was not worth the outcome.

As more Europeans flocked to the West for various economic purposes including mining, logging, and agriculture, bighorns faced increased hunting pressure and habitat loss. In the late nineteenth century, bighorn sheep were pursued by market hunters who sold their meat and hides. However, death by disease transmitted from domestic sheep to bighorns was probably more instrumental in the widespread collapse of bighorn sheep populations that occurred across the western United States from the late 1800s to around 1960. In Idaho, for example, ranchers introduced domestic sheep by the thousands in the 1860s and 1870s. Shortly thereafter, homesteaders witnessed massive die-offs of bighorns in the central part of the state to the extent that

Domestic sheep graze on an alpine ridge in Colorado. Diseases from domestic sheep have been implicated in numerous die-offs of bighorns that led to population collapses in the late eighteenth century. SHUTTERSTOCK

the bones of sheep were scattered across their winter range for several decades. A similar pattern plagued bighorns in many other Rocky Mountain states. Oregon was historically home to bighorns, but disease reduced their numbers to less than fifty animals by around 1910. The feeble population rallied slightly in subsequent decades, but by the mid-1940s the species had vanished from the state.

Around 1900 most states passed legislation prohibiting the hunting of bighorn sheep. But the species continued to languish due to habitat loss and disease outbreaks. Bighorn sheep persisted in the high mountains of Colorado into the twentieth century, but experienced one of the most dramatic die-offs in the post-settlement era in the United States. In 1953 disease swept through one of the largest herds. A single winter saw sheep numbers in the region (central Colorado) plunge from around 1,000 to 30, representing a population decline of roughly 97 percent in a period of a few months.

Bighorns and Us

The plight of the desert bighorn sheep received substantial publicity in 1936 when Boy Scouts in Arizona began a program aimed at preserving bighorns. Major Frederick Russell Burnham, an outspoken conservationist, became concerned that less than 200 bighorns persisted in the mountains of Arizona. Burnham enlisted the help of Boy Scout leaders to spread the word about the magnificent sheep and their precarious existence. A poster contest with a "save the bighorns" theme was conducted in schools across the state. The winning entry was used on a special neckerchief slide distributed to some 10,000 Scouts. Other publicity efforts included radio programs and school assemblies documenting the plight of the state's bighorns.

Conservation efforts by the Boy Scouts of America in Arizona in the 1930s led to the creation of two national wildlife refuges intended to protect bighorn sheep.

SHUTTERSTOCK

Several prominent national conservation groups including the Izaak Walton League of America, the National Audubon Society, and the National Wildlife Federation rallied to the cause. As a result, two national wildlife refuges were created in Arizona with the specific intention to conserve habitat for desert bighorn sheep and other wildlife. The total area of the refuges (Kofa and Cabeza Prieta) covers 1.5 million acres, or 23,437 square miles. In 2012 the desert bighorn population in the smaller Kofa refuge was estimated at nearly 500 animals.

Efforts to reestablish bighorn sheep on their native range began as early as 1922, when South Dakota senator Peter Norbeck acquired eight bighorns from Canada that were released in Custer State Park. The same year, Canadian bighorns were released in Montana on the National Bison Range. Bighorns were transplanted in New Mexico from Canada in 1932. In Colorado, native bighorn sheep numbers were sufficient to provide seed stock for transplant efforts elsewhere in the state. Sheep captured in the Tarryall Mountains (a sub-range of the Front Range) were moved to the Mount Evans area in 1945. In the next seven years, 223 bighorns from the Tarryall Mountains were relocated to thirteen other sites in Colorado. The transplants were timely. The 1953 disease epidemic (referenced above) that virtually wiped out Tarryall's bighorns put an end to the transplant program from the Tarryall population, but animals from many of the previous transplants thrived in their new environments.

Across the western United States, transplant programs returned bighorns to native range in many areas in the 1960s and 1970s. Since that time, relocation efforts have remained active. Numerous transplants have been successful, resulting in growing bighorn populations of both the desert and Rocky Mountain subspecies. However, acute disease outbreaks continue to plague bighorns in many places. As noted in chapter 6, a high percentage of these are known or suspected to originate from contact with domestic sheep. Young bighorn rams are sometimes seen investigating domestic sheep herds, and individual domestic sheep occasionally wind up in odd places on bighorn sheep range.

CARNAGE FROM CARS

Accidents claim the lives of bighorn sheep in numerous habitats. Bighorns have drowned in the Colorado River and been struck by trains. The skeleton of a young ram was found in Nevada, its horns encircling a cable. Sheep occasionally fall from cliffs or become trapped in sinkholes.

In some places collisions with automobiles claim disturbing numbers of wild bighorns. One research project near Hoover Dam in Arizona focused on forty-nine adult animals. During the study period, twelve sheep were killed. Six of the mortalities occurred when bighorns were struck by automobiles, a full 50 percent of the mortality, accounting for exactly twice as many deaths as predation.

A substantial herd of bighorns inhabits the area around Georgetown, Colorado, adjacent to I-90 and other roads. Vehicle collisions have claimed many bighorns from the Georgetown herd, where biologists once witnessed the death of five bighorn rams in a single vehicle accident.

Bighorn/automobile collisions have also claimed substantial numbers of sheep in Montana. A single week in the summer of 2013 saw seven bighorns killed by vehicles in three different locations. From 2008 to 2012, 107 bighorns were killed in the Thompson Falls area. Biologists concluded mortality from motor vehicle accidents during the period was instrumental in an overall decline of sheep population in the area. A 2012 vehicle incident in the Rock Creek drainage east of Missoula, where bighorn sheep were recovering from a 2010 pneumonia outbreak, killed seven bighorn lambs in a single collision. The lambs represented a full one-third of the year's reproduction within the struggling population.

Management response to vehicle accidents that may claim human life as well as bighorns is growing.

State wildlife agencies and highway departments have increased signage and protected crossings for bighorns in many locations. Motorists can do their part by heeding signs and slowing their travels where highways and sheep habitat intersect.

Collisions with automobiles claim substantial numbers of bighorn sheep in some areas. Signs, such as this one in Arches National Park, Utah, notify motorists that bighorns may be on the road. SHUTTERSTOCK

Transplants in the nineteenth century accounted for the recovery of bighorn populations in many areas, including Badlands National Park in South Dakota. Relocation of bighorns continues to this day, and is an important part of sheep management. SHUTTERSTOCK

During a severe disease epidemic in Colorado in the Tarryall and Kenosha Mountains that began in 1997, a single domestic sheep was discovered among a band of bighorns in remote habitat. The domestic sheep was promptly removed, but numerous bighorn mortalities due to pneumonia occurred in the vicinity where the domestic sheep was discovered. Natural interchange between bighorns was suspected of transmitting the disease to other sheep in the area. The final result was a loss of approximately 50 percent of the bighorns in the two mountain ranges.

Successful recovery programs have shown that new bighorn sheep populations can be established in suitable habitat. But the vulnerability of wild sheep to pneumonia and other diseases and habitat loss or disturbance appears more acute than with other North American ungulates. Funding for transplant programs and bighorn research is an essential component of the continued health of the species. The greatest share of funding for sheep management and research comes from state wildlife agencies, primarily in the form of revenue from hunting licenses and excise taxes on the sale of sporting equipment including firearms, ammunition, archery tackle, and arrows. Several conservation organizations devoted to bighorn sheep have also been instrumental in funding transplant programs, habitat improvement projects, and research. Hunters comprise the majority of membership in such organizations.

Some commentators have suggested that a broader investment by state and federal governments, not so heavily dependent on hunting dollars, is warranted for bighorn sheep conservation. Whatever the sources, bighorn sheep are a unique and valuable species worthy of considerable economic and management investment to ensure their future survival.

Index

Index

About the Author

A writer, photographer, and naturalist, Jack Ballard is a frequent contributor to numerous regional and national publications. He has written hundreds of articles on wildlife and wildlife-related topics. His photos have been published in numerous books (Smithsonian Press, Heinemann Library, etc.), calendars, and magazines.

Jack has received multiple awards for his writing and photography from the Outdoor Writers Association of America and other professional organizations. He holds two master's degrees and is an accomplished public speaker, entertaining students, conference attendees, and recreation/conservation groups with his compelling narratives. When not wandering the backcountry, he hangs his hat in Red Lodge, Montana. See more of his work at jackballard.com.